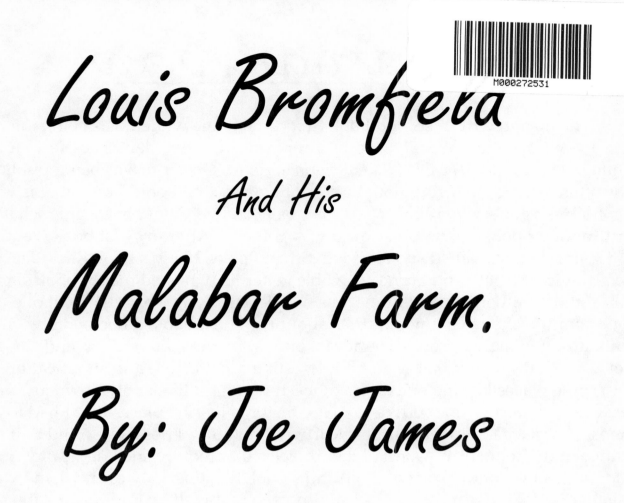

Louis Bromfield

And His

Malabar Farm,

By: Joe James

First Edition: 2013
Printed in the United States of America
ISBN 978-0-615-76658-4

Introduction

The idea to write a second book first came to me while I was being interviewed by a TV news station, WMFD, and by a reporter from the Mansfield News Journal while my first book, *The Ohio State Reformatory: An Overview* was being publicized. I was often asked "have you thought of writing a second book?" or "what is your second book going to be about?" At first, I sincerely did not have a clue what I could write another book about, or if I even was going to. After my first book went on sale, many stores in Mansfield such as Main Street Books, Holly's Book Rack, The Ohio Genealogical Society and Barnes & Noble generously hosted me for book signings. It was at those gatherings that numerous people asked me what "the next one was going to be about." After so many inquiries about my "next book" I decided it was time to evaluate some places in and around not only Mansfield, but in Richland County as well. I was intrigued by places with interesting architecture and significant history, with some places lacking one or the other. It was hard to narrow down just one place because Richland County offers so many historically rich places that I had to dwell on choosing a place to write about for nearly two months: I possess a mind that likes to change quite frequently, especially on projects that require such dedication for an extended period of time, such as writing a book like this. However, when I went to Malabar Farm, I discovered a place and person that I felt I could relate with very well. This intrigued me to conduct more research, which in turn lead to me relating more to this person and his home life. Although its founder, Louis Bromfield, is long deceased, I found the man and his home very easy and enjoyable to relate to. I began doing research and listening to stories from park naturalists and my family members (some who remember visiting Malabar in their younger years when Louis and his family lived there). It has worked out that I am fortunate enough to be related to the family who built Louis Bromfield's desk in his office/bedroom, and also the fruit stand, that still stands beside the Malabar Inn today. The sons of the man who built these relics shared stories of how Mr. Bromfield gave them a boxer dog to express his appreciation of their father's outstanding workmanship.

After hearing so many stories from so many people, related and not, I became fascinated by how much I could relate to someone who was known around the world because of how diverse he was with his interests, professions, and skills. I have become particularly fond of how Mr. Bromfield could be in the field during the day with a flannel shirt, pants, and boots wading in cow and pig manure, then by night time he could be hosting a house with six to ten guests and be wining and dining with the finest foods and drinks. Perhaps he provided such generous hospitality to people whom he had met just eight hours before because they came to visit him at his home and farm.

I can also relate with Mr. Bromfield and his passionate love for dogs. I am fortunate to have three wonderful dogs. My first one, Gus, is a West Highland White Terrier and provides me with the most company of the three, which is fine because he is the most pleasant. The second dog, Chester, is a Brussels Griffon whose breed originates from Belgium. He is very 'talkative' if you will. However he is very alert and makes a great watchdog. The third dog, Charlie, is a small rather curious, yet cautious dog. He is a Yorkie-Chon, and as his name indicates he is a mix between a Yorkshire Terrier and a Bichon-Frise. Every so often when I am writing for the local newspaper, *The Bellville Star,* or when I am working on my books, I get a visit from Gus, who nudges the door and opens it for a late night visit, usually when the other dogs are asleep.

Another thing that intrigues me about Mr. Bromfield is how he could be working with the farmer down the road on his plow or manure spreader during the day then by the end of the night he might be talking to a farmer he met from Brazil. Even though I do not possess the extravagant goals of agriculture that Mr. Bromfield did, I often enjoy working outside in the chicken house and in the spring I work the ground of the garden. In the summer our piece of property produces lavish (both quantity and quality) elderberries, black raspberries, red raspberries, and mulberries. Several trees such as sassafras and apple, which grow in abundance on our property, give us the opportunity to share and consume organic produce with our friends and family. I keep a close eye on the produce that our property naturally produces. Also I gather eggs from the chicken house and share them with family. During the Ohio winter season, the property keeps me busy with having to clean up fallen timber, cleaning the sidewalks for the dogs so they may have a place to walk, (as the tallest is only approximately eight inches from the ground). Keeping the driveway clear of snow can sometimes be a daily job.

I can also relate to Mr. Bromfield in the aspects that we both can 'blend' into the environments that we subject ourselves to. We do that based on our professions, interests, or things we are passionate about. I found that I have the skill to be able to blend with several different groups just as Mr. Bromfield did. Whether he was speaking with politicians, farmers, or Hollywood screen writers, he had the clothes, vocabulary, and knowledge to fit in with any of those groups while offering a valuable opinion and wise words. My skill of blending is becoming better as I broaden my interests and subject myself to different people. Currently I find myself mixing with people of two different walks of life; fortunately both honor and value my words and opinion. I suppose this ability will become better with age and experience. I am, however, very fortunate to have these people in my life who help me sharpen these skills. A few very important aspects of my life are the criticism I get from my works, the company of my friends and the support they give me, and the drive and inspiration I receive from my family. I have been told I take criticism very well and I think if you wish to do better in what you enjoy doing, you have to take it well, because if you do not, then you will let yourself be get 'put-down' and not have the ambition to do any better. With the criticism I get from the generous people who purchase and read my books I absorb it, and keep it in mind while writing the next book, because if I keep the criticism in mind it inspires me and tells me what to make better. If it weren't for my parents, grandparents, aunts, uncles, cousins, and siblings, I might not have been able to compose my first book, or this one, as they inspire me to keep writing and they drive me to do better with each thing I write, whether it is for publication or self satisfaction.

During the pre-production stages of this book I received the unfortunate news that the life of my best friend had been taken. To me the news was very disheartening and initially surreal. I actually got this news at a celebration I was attending at the location of my first book, The Ohio State Reformatory, on the evening of Saturday, December 17, 2011. After the candle light vigil and funeral, the closure fortunately did not take long for me to grasp. Looking back on our friendship, Nick Gaumer, was someone who would always help me when I needed it. He would always inspire me and encourage me to do my best and never let anyone tell me I couldn't do any better than that. I could write a book on why he was the best friend anyone could ask for, as I am sure you could about your closest friend too, but I am not. In recognition of the things he has done for me, I would like to dedicate this book, the labor, and time it has taken to compose it, to him and the things he shared with me. Between the valuable lessons he taught me, and the memories we made, and his overall generosity, common courtesy, positive attitude, and his charismatic personality that he enveloped everyone with, I feel that dedicating a book is the least I can do to show my gratitude towards the things he did for me and for everyone with whom he became acquainted. Even though, now in heaven, Nick has remained a big inspiration in the completion of this book and in my daily life. I keep a picture of him and me on my desk at where I write, for when the research becomes extensive and the writers block decides to plague me for a short while, I look at the picture and think of what he would tell me, and then I am right back to writing. I would like to express my appreciation to a few people who have had a key role in the production in this book. The first person I would like to express my sincere thanks to is my close friend, Matt Davies. Matt selflessly made time in his busy schedule to work with me.

I can be particularly finicky at times with projects such as this. Matt is responsible for how well the cover looks. As you read about George Hawkins in this book, Matt Davies is a George Hawkins to me. A close friend, sometimes business partner, and an honest critic of the things I do. Matt leads me in the right direction, much like George did for Louis Bromfield. Susan Nirode edited my last book, but due to occupation changes she has moved out of state and cannot edit this one. Susan was very knowledgeable of the reformatory, and great with English composition and grammar, but she can not be part of this project. I would like to thank her in this book for providing such great assistance with my last book, as well as Ted Morrison and Michael Humphrey who were also of great assistance. The entire staff at Malabar Farm has been very instrumental in providing me with a great abundance of knowledge of the Bromfield family, Malabar Farm and everything on it. Their hospitality included complimentary tours, taking the time out of their busy days to help me when I showed up unannounced, to access newspaper articles and their archives. The local media has played a key role in the success of the books I write. They always show great interest in the historical locations around Richland County about which I write. I would like to thank WMFD, WVNO, WMAN, "The Mansfield News Journal", "The Bellville Star", The Mansfield/Richland County Convention and Visitors Bureau, "Heart of Ohio Magazine", "North Central Ohio Events Magazine", and many others for the publicity they have given my works and me. If people like you didn't take the time to read my books, if people like you didn't write to me and give me reviews on my books, if people like you did not purchase my books, and the others I have mentioned, I would not write them. I would not pursue the goals I have pursued and I would not have accomplished the things I have. Thank you for doing so. If you do not think I am being sincere about this, please continue to doubt me and e-mail me at LBJJBook@yahoo.com so I can get to know you and express my thanks by a handwritten letter, mailed to your address of choice and signed personally by me. While people still continue to ask me about writing in my future, I still answer the same, "I will continue to write as long as the demand for the books are there, but I will not pursue it as a career unless I get asked to do so. Until then, I will only compose books on the basis of people wanting me to keep doing so, and for my pleasure." If so many people had not supported me in my first book, this book would not have been published. I hope you enjoy reading my second book, *Louis Bromfield and his Malabar Farm.* Your opinion and criticism matters to me, so please feel free to e-mail me at the address above. I would love to hear your thoughts about the book. I sincerely hope you enjoy this book and gather enjoyment from the photographs and words in this book on which I have spent over a year composing. Thank you for reading the introduction to this book. You are about to read a book that will enlighten you on the Bromfield lifestyle and how one of the most revolutionary and famous farms in America operated and how one of America's most famous authors, politicians and soil conservationists operated it, and who helped him. Since you have taken the time to read the introduction, I ask that you take the time to read the forward, genuinely written by my close friend, and business partner, Greg Seiter. I hope you enjoy my book and gather useful information.

Yours Truthfully,

Joe James

Forward

I have known Joe James now for about 6 years. He was a confident young man that was not afraid to let his thoughts and views to be expressed. At the time I was teaching a freshman high school science class and he was one of my new students. Joe made his self at home in my classroom and the next four years seemed to fly by.

My grandmother was also a science teacher and she had told me that one day a student will come into my class and they will seem different from the rest. Her prophecy came true when I first met Joe. Over the next few weeks Joe proved he was not a typical 14 year old student and this could be narrowed down to one attribute, charisma.

I have tried over the last 6 years to mentor him and let him know the power of charisma. When he was in my class as a teacher aide we would do some scientific experiments with his charisma. We would sit at my desk and the students would just gather around my desk before and after classes. Students rather than use their time wisely and do their assignments; Joe's charisma just drew them in. Then Joe would sit to the back of the classroom and the students would gravitate there. He then would laugh and say that "I must really have that charisma stuff". This makes Joe an extra special human being. I have been in business now with Joe since his graduation from school. With his no hold bars attitude and that great charisma he can go along way. Another thing about Joe is he really believes in what he does. He loves the local history of Mansfield, Ohio and the surrounding communities. This is his second book and I am sure if one has read his first they will not be disappointed in this one.

Joe you are a good friend, keep up the good work,

Gregory L. Seiter

IN MEMORY & DEDICATION OF:
NICHOLAS MICHAEL GAUMER.

"LOVE MUST BE SINCERE
HATE WHAT IS EVIL; CLING TO WHAT IS GOOD."
~ROMANS 12:9
(This was one of Nick's favorite versus.)

12.17.11 ... That date will forever pierce our hearts, every breath and our souls. For 16 years, 9 months and 9 hours, WE were blessed to Live, Laugh, and Love with Nicholas Michael Gaumer (or Nick, as we called him). As Nick grew, his talents and interests became true and defined. He was a star runner (Track & Cross Country) for the Fredericktown Jr. & Sr. High School teams. As a talented horseman, Nick competed and excelled in speed events (he particularly loved Barrels and Flags). Nick also enjoyed hunting, golfing and the times spent with his 4H Club and the FUMC Youth Group. His passions were many and when Nick committed to something, he gave no less than HIS ALL. Many would agree, Nick's infectious personality was complimented by his smile, his zest for life and his craving for Mountain Dew and Snickers bars. In his quieter moments, Nick could usually be found reading. It seems very fitting that Nick's friend, Joe, has dedicated this book to our Angel.

Thank you, Joe, and to all who contributed to the quality of life that Nick was blessed to have enjoyed during his short time here.

~Mike & Carrie Gaumer.

The heart hands mural was painted by ...... in honor of Nick in December 2011. Nick was known for his hand hearts.

The Bromfield Years: 1896-1913

Lewis Brumfield's grand parents, Thomas Dalton Brumfield and Margret Jane Wise were the parents of his father, Charles Brumfield. Thomas was born on November 11, 1828 and passed away on November 21, 1911. His wife, Margret was born on March 16, 1839 and passed away on September 13, 1891. His grandparents on his mother's side were Robert Coulter and Adelaide Barr Coulter and they were the parents to Louis' mom, Annette Marie Coulter. Lewis' father's name was Charles Brumfield and he was born on January 2, 1863 and he passed away on April 23, 1944. His mother's name was Annette Marie Coulter Brumfield and she was born on April 2, 1864 and she passed away on January 7, 1947. They had their first child, a girl, Marie Coulter Brumfield on August 13, 1886; she passed away on July 14, 1936. On December 22, 1900 they had their second child, Charles Brumfield Jr. On December 27, 1896 at 323 West Third St. in Mansfield, Ohio, Charles and Annette Coulter Bromfield welcomed their last son, Lewis Brucker Brumfield. Lewis' mother, Annette, is the one who often inspired Lewis to write and she often encouraged him to fulfill his dreams and goals. His mother was a writer and inspired Lewis in his early life to write and to go on the pursuit to attain a higher education after high school. Lewis' father, Charles was a farmer in his early life and taught Lewis the trades of farming. Later in life Charles went into the business of buying and selling real estate. He then retired as a real estate salesman.

Lewis attended Mansfield Senior High School. It is rumored that Lewis would go to school smelling like a cow pasture and with mud on his boots. Lewis graduated under the name he was born with, Lewis Brumfield. When one of Lewis' early works got published, his last name was misspelled "Bromfield". After Lewis saw the mistake, he liked the way it sounded so much that he decided to have it legally changed and it stuck with him for his entire life.

"In any case there is a great job to be done in the field of agriculture from one end of the world to the other."
~ Louis Bromfield.

The Bromfield Years: 1914-1919

Louis graduated from Mansfield Senior High School in 1914. In three of the four high school annuals, Louis' name is spelled Lewis Brumfield, all besides his senior annual. While Louis was growing up his father was a struggling farmer. His mother encouraged him to further his knowledge and education so that he would not have the troubles providing for his family that his father did. When Louis was eighteen years old he enrolled at Cornell University in New York to study agriculture. After studying agriculture for approximately a year he returned to Ohio to help his father on the family farm. Bromfield then decided to change his major to journalism. In 1916, after being back home for only one year, he then decided to enroll at Columbia University. Bromfield would soon become part of the fraternal organization, Phi Delta Theta. The three primary objectives of this fraternal organization are the cultivation of friendship among its members, the acquirement individually of a high degree of mental culture, and the attainment personally of a high standard of morality. In a little under a year, Bromfield would become bored with his college studies and would enlist in the United States Army on June 6, 1917. Shortly after enlisting Bromfield got transferred to Europe on December 26, 1917. He arrived in Europe on January 13, 1918, to drive an ambulance for the Section Sanitaire American Number 557, American Field Service. It was not until 1919 that Bromfield would return to the United States. In recognition of serving in seven major battles, Bromfield was later awarded the Croix de guerre. This medal is an award given to those who served in a foreign allied country of the United States and perform acts of courage or heroism. Bromfield was awarded the medal by the country of France.

"If the whole of the younger generation is as good, the future of the country is safe."
~Louis Bromfield.

The Bromfield Years: 1919-1921

On May 23, 1919 Louis left Europe and he arrived in New York on June 14, 1919. Before he returned to the United States he explored the French countryside and studied their farming techniques. Louis was formally discharged from the Army on June 11, 1919. What Louis had seen in his early years in France would change the way he would lead the rest of his life. After Louis returned he found work in New York City as a reporter for several publications such as *Time Magazine, Musical America, New York City News Service,* and the Associated Press. Bromfield also worked as a magazine editor, a critic, an assistant to a theatrical producer, and as an advertising manager for the book publishing company, Putnam. While working in New York Louis met his future wife, Mary Appleton Wood. Mary was born on May 30, 1892 in Ipswich, Massachusetts to Chalmers and Ellen Cotton Smith Wood. Due to her family's prominent background (her father, a lawyer, and her cousin, a police commissioner in New York), Mary was provided a secure lifestyle. Mary enjoyed lavish parties, and due to her father's exceptional income, he let the expensive and frequent parties become a regular part of Mary's routine life. An excerpt from *The New York Times* suggests that Mary may have partied a lot in her younger years. At the age of 19 Mary was issued her second summons by the local courts for tearing up her first one when it was given to her. When the Magistrate heard of this, he issued her a second one.

"In simple words we farmed too much land in order to produce the record of food production we attained."
~Louis Bromfield.

The Bromfield Years: 1921-1927

Mr. Bromfield and Miss Wood got married in Wood's hometown on October 12, 1921 at the Ascension Memorial Church. Wood's uncle, Reverend Roland Cotton Smith conducted the ceremony, while Wood's brother, Reverend William Lawrence Wood, assisted. Louis' brother, Charles Bromfield Jr., served as best man while Chalmers Wood Jr. and Guy Emerson served as ushers for the event. Three years later, in 1924, one of Bromfield's best sellers was published; it was entitled *The Green Bay Tree*. After his book was published Louis and Mary moved to Cold Spring Harbor, Long Island, New York. Shortly after, in the same year, on June 6, 1925, the Bromfields had their first daughter, Anne Chalmers Bromfield. It was after Anne's birth and the success of his book that Bromfield would start writing full time. The Bromfields also left the United States and ventured to France in 1925 for a vacation. The vacation was only supposed to be a month long but eventually would turn into a nearly thirteen year long stay. The Bromfield family would end up residing in a French Villa in the village of Senlis. The family fell so in love with the French countryside and way of life that they took a fifty year lease on their home in Senlis. In 1925 Bromfield released *Possession*. While the Bromfields resided in France, Louis wrote and published 14 works, which included the book that won him the Pulitzer Prize in 1927, *Early Autumn* (published in 1926). The Pulitzer Prize is given by what would have been Louis' Alma mater, Columbia University to authors, poets, and composers who excel in newspaper journalism, literary achievements, and musical compositions. Winners receive prizes such as cash awards and national recognition. In 1927 Bromfield published *A Good Woman*, and his first play, *The House of Women*. Mr. Bromfield published all these works while living in Senlis. After winning the Pulitzer Prize Louis returned to America and accepted his award.

"What I am trying to say is that the farmer, the good farmer, has in a starving world become an increasingly important and vital citizen."
~ Louis Bromfield.

The Bromfield Years: 1927-1934

While in America, Louis accepted a position at a commercial lecturing enterprise and traveled throughout the United States, before returning to France upon the completion of his contract. One year later in France Louis wrote *The Strange Case of Miss Annie Spragg*. The next year, in 1929, Bromfield published his first collection of short stories, *Awake and Rehearse*. Also in 1929, Bromfield published *The Scarlet Women*, which would win him third place in the O. Henry Short Story Award; Bromfield received $100 in prize money. After hearing of Bromfield's success, Samuel Goldwyn of MGM offered to pay Bromfield $2,500 dollars a week to write for him. Bromfield accepted the offer and came back to the United States to write. Anxious to get back to France, Bromfield bought out his contract for $10,000 dollars and tried to finish up his work in the states. Later that year, on June 27, 1929, the Bromfields had their second daughter, Mary Hope Bromfield. This was a very crucial year for Bromfield as he met George Hawkins, who would become his long time friend, business manager, and editor for his works and projects. A year later in 1930, Bromfield published and released rights to Paramount Studios for *Twenty-Four Hours*. Bromfield would also work on his next series of short stories, *Tabloid News*. Later that year Bromfield returned to France to his wife and now, two children. On April 25, 1932, Mary and Louis had their third daughter, Ellen Margret Bromfield. Bromfield also published and sold rights to Warner Brothers for his publication, *A Modern Hero*. In 1933, Bromfield published one of his better known novels, *The Farm* and started to publicly talk about his dreams of owning his own farm either in the United States or on the Malabar Coast of India. Bromfield only published one work in 1934 and it was *Here Today and Gone Tomorrow*.

"I rose and walked out of my room, which is on the ground floor, onto the terrace to *feel* the rain."
~ Louis Bromfield.

The Bromfield Years: 1935-1942

In 1935 Bromfield traveled to India, particularly to the Malabar Coast. He stayed there for three months. In 1935 he published *The Man Who Had Everything,* and his second play, *Times Have Changed.* In June of 1937 Harper Brothers published one of Bromfield's most well known novels that would eventually be turned into a motion picture film, *The Rains Came.* In 1938 with tensions of World War II rising and becoming a greater threat in France, Louis sent his wife and three daughters back to the United States and promised he would join them soon. In time, he returned to the United States as he promised, and that ended the Bromfield's thirteen year rendezvous in France. In 1939 he found three separate farms in the town of Lucas, Ohio and purchased them all. Bromfield would then combine them all, and call them collectively, Malabar Farm. During his first year back in the United States, 1939, he published another collection of short stories, *It Takes All Kinds.* Later that year Bromfield published his first of three books in the political/economic genre; it was entitled *England, A Dying Oligarchy.* In 1940, Bromfield published *Night In Bombay.* Later that year Bromfield hired architect Louis Lameroux who would begin work on designing the Bromfield's new home, The Big House. In the mean time Louis, Mary, and their daughters, Anne, Hope, and Ellen lived in a house on an adjacent property, which was a Sears and Roebuck catalog house. Later in the year Louis purchased a fourth farm to add to his Malabar Farm. Even though living in a temporary home, Louis was still active in organizing a protest group of about 700 other farmers, who refused to produce wheat if the government won a law suit on wheat quota. Louis only published one work this year and it was titled *Wild Is The River.*

"In the woods there was a warm, steamy mist coming up from the decaying leaves. It smelled of decay and fungus and the promise of new life."
~ Louis Bromfield.

The Bromfield Years: 1942-1945

In 1942 the family moved into The Big House at Bromfield's dream farm, Malabar. Louis also published his twentieth piece entitled *Until The Day Break*. The first book Louis published while living at Malabar was *Mrs. Parkington*. In 1944 Bromfield went on a nation wide bond selling tour and described it as "tough work, but worth it not only because our team of speakers sold millions of dollars worth of bonds, but because we saw, met and talked with so many different kinds of people in so many different cities.", as he said in the *Berkeley Daily Gazette* on February 19, 1944. On April 23, 1944 Charles Bromfield Sr., Louis' dad, passed away at Louis' home. In 1944 Bromfield published *What Became Of Anna Bolton* and *The World We Live In*. On October 7, 1945 Bromfield wrote an article that appeared in *The Miami News*, protesting the draft because he insisted that "there are signs that Selective Service is reviving its old trick of raiding the farms for new recruits for the army." Also in that year he published *Pleasant Valley*. In May of that year Bromfield's friend Humphrey Bogart married his fourth wife, Lauren Bacall at Louis Bromfield's now world famous, Malabar Farm. Even though the couple got married on May 21, 1945, their marriage license was issued a day before the wedding by Judge Herbert Schettler, who also oversaw the wedding. Flowers from Bromfield's farm were used to decorate the Big House for the ceremony. Louis was Bogart's first man for his fourth wedding, while Bromfield's manager and friend, George Hawkins, gave the bride away. When Bacall and Bogart got married, she was 20 years old and he was 45 years old. Louis and his wife, Mary, went to the train station to get Mr. Bogart and Ms. Bacall and drove them back to the farm where they would stay. On the day of the wedding local authorities blocked the entrance to the home as Ms. Bacall wanted the event to be strictly private. Press was allowed in for a half an hour to cover the event but had to leave once the wedding started.

"I like political speeches and talking to farmers and businessmen and to people who share common interests."
~ Louis Bromfield.

The Bromfield Years: 1945-1949

In January of 1945 Louis purchased a telephone company. As elaborate as it may sound, during an interview Bromfield stated "it's not so hot." Locals enjoyed picking up the phone line to listen what the author was talking about and with whom. The year before Bacall and Bogart were to get married, locals would often hear Bromfield talking with Bacall or Bogart about the wedding and with other people who Bromfield knew from around the world. In 1946 Bromfield was instrumental in orchestrating the American Writer's Association, which was supposed to "prevent a monopoly control over all American literary production." Later that year Bromfield published his second political/economical book, *A Few Brass Tacks*. In 1947 Bromfield's sixth book in his collection of short stories is published; it is called *Kenny*. Bromfield also released his seventeenth novel *Colorado* in the same year. Unfortunately, just three years after losing his father, Bromfield also lost his mother on January 7, 1947 as she passed away in her sleep at Malabar. Just one year later, in 1948, Louis also lost his long-time best friend, business partner and editor, George Hawkins, who died of a heart attack at the Hotel St. Regis in New York City. Hawkins' bedroom at Malabar was designed to look like his favorite room at the St. Regis. In the midst of his mother's, and best friend's death Bromfield managed to publish *The Wild Country* and *Malabar Farm*. In 1949 Bromfield, now without parents or an editor and business partner would try and tackle "The Butter vs. Margarine Battle" in Congress. Bromfield stated that "the unrestricted sale of yellow margarine would increase the acreage planted to the soil-depleting crops of cotton and soy beans, from which margarine is produced." Bromfield was testifying on behalf of the Andersen Bill, which would have wiped out federal margarine taxes, and also would have banned the sale of yellow margarine all together.

"Ma, my mother, is extraordinary. At eighty-three she takes the liveliest and most intelligent interest in everything that goes on at Malabar. . ."
~ Louis Bromfield.

The Bromfield Years: 1950-1956

After having his battle with the government about butter, Bromfield published *Out of The Earth,* in 1950. His daughter, Hope, got married at Malabar while his other daughter, Ellen, got married two weeks later in New York. In the summer of that year, Bromfield worked with a group of 15 other people (which included scientist, Albert Einstein) to urge the United States to take part in a disarmament program put together by the National Council Against Conscription.

In the early fifties, Bromfield spent a lot of time considering and thinking about where he wanted to make another Malabar Farm. Several years earlier, in 1949, Bromfield was granted a deed to a 411 acre farm in Wichita Falls, Texas. Bromfield claimed that it had been ruined by over-irrigation to the ground, erosion, and over - grazing. In 1954, the Wichita Falls Chamber opened a law suit against Bromfield and his associates which claimed that Bromfield and his associates did not live up to contract on restoring the farm land, and that the land should revert to the ownership of the chamber. Bromfield's attorneys claimed that the chamber did not cooperate with Bromfield or his management at the farm. In 1951, Bromfield published *Mr. Smith.* In September of 1952 his wife, Mary, passed away at Malabar Farm in her room. In 1953, Bromfield became a consultant for Malabar do-Brasil, a Brazilian farming operation comparable to the Malabar in Ohio. His daughter, Ellen, and husband, Carson, became farm managers. In 1954, Bromfield published, *A New Pattern For a Tired World.* In 1955, Bromfield published his last two works, *Animals and Other People,* and *From My Experience.* Bromfield collapsed at Malabar Farm in February of 1956, and passed away on March 18, at a hospital in Columbus, after hiding his bone marrow cancer condition from everyone for nearly a year. He was 59 years old.

"I have had much to be thankful for in my personal life and the life of Malabar, most of all the great progress that has been made during the last year. . ."
~Louis Bromfield.

Malabar Dissected

The previous section viewed Louis Bromfield's life, from the aspects of his achievements and literary works, along with his goals and dreams. The next section will dissect his dream farm, Malabar. We will take a further look into Bromfield's methods of farming, and things he did around the farm. We will also go where he and his guests would enjoy each others' company, as well as where Bromfield would write his books, and where he would spend time with his wife, daughters, and what sometimes seemed to be so important to Mr. Bromfield, his boxers.

"The business of soil conservation, of checking run-off water and erosion is becoming generally accepted and is being more and more widely practiced. The next stage is soil restoration—the restoration of both organic materials and minerals. Until all this is understood and practiced our American agriculture will continue to be wasteful and extravagant. Our food costs will continue to mount and the farmer's margin of profit to decrease."
~Louis Bromfield.

When Louis returned to the United States from France with his family, he knew he wanted to purchase a farm to initially make self-sustaining. The farm would later be used as a place to conduct studies and experiments, as well as a place to settle and raise a family; a place he could call home. When he and his family returned to his hometown of Mansfield, Ohio, Louis found just what he had envisioned. Louis made Mr. Herring an offer he couldn't refuse on his farm the same day that he saw it. What he found would change his life forever. It was a small farm in Lucas, Ohio with several pastures and a small house. Eventually Louis would purchase three more adjacent farms with several barns, pastures, ponds, and what he wanted most, worn out land. He would call all 643 acres of farm land, Malabar Farm. Malabar Farm was named after the Malabar Coast of India, where Bromfield vacationed for several months while living in Europe. Above the main entrance of the big house is a sculpture of the Hindu Lord of Success, Ganesha.

"In a way, although there were plans and blueprints, the Big House was built the way a house should be built, bit by bit as we went along."
~Louis Bromfield.

Louis Bromfield had the intention of building a home with the idea that every family member would design his or her own room to add a nice variety of colors, carpets, wallpapers, and overall look and feel for the Big House. While building the Big House, Bromfield worked closely with architect, Louis Lameroux, who was familiar with the Ohio countryside. Louis Lameroux also had the help from I.T. Frary, of the Cleveland Museum, who helped him in fulfilling Bromfield's needs of a home that would represent the architectural style of The Jefferson Greek Revival and Western Reserve styles of architecture. Bromfield described this room below, as the purest example of Jefferson Greek revival. He attributes this to the matching staircases and niches in the walls at either landing of the stairs, and the large hall way that runs through the room, and large doors that can enclose the room. The red couches were purchased in New York City and are original to the Bromfield family.

"I possess, unfortunately, a hopelessly unmechanical mind with an utter inability to understand blueprints or to visualize from blueprints the final result."
~Louis Bromfield.

The Bromfields were a large, lively family of five. The family was very popular in France as Bromfield established himself as a young American author on the rise. The Bromfields, like they would in America, enjoyed wining, dining, and socializing with an upper class of people in France, as well as the middle and lower classes. This level of satisfaction and space is something Bromfield demanded his home in America be able to provide for him and his guests. He enjoyed staying up well into the night with his guests. His daughters, Hope and Ellen, also developed this mentality as they would have friends over almost every weekend and entertain them as well. Louis enjoyed having friends over on the weekends as well, to entertain and converse most of the time over world affairs, farming techniques and politics.

"We had countless elements to consider. One thing was that we were a family of *big* people, big physically and rather big and loose and careless in our living."
~Louis Bromfield.

From her prominent background, as explained earlier in the book, Mary Bromfield took extreme pleasure in entertaining guests at the Big House. She insisted that the Big House be decorated in such a manner that it would bring the best out of everyone who entered, and Louis agreed. To help encourage their guests to have a better experience at their home, Mary had her initials embossed on her cutlery, dinnerware, and had them embroidered on her linen napkins. The dinner table pictured below was brought to their home in the United States from their home in Senlis, France. The dining table is from the 1750s. The cabinet on the far right of the room also came from the Bromfield's home in Senlis. It was crafted in the 1750's as well. The chandelier also held a special place in the Bromfield's home in Senlis, so special that they had to have it at the Big House as well. The Bromfields brought home three full train boxcar loads of furnishings.

"Our house is a big house, well built, to be used not only by ourselves but by friends and neighbors as well..."
~Louis Bromfield.

After Mr. Bromfield established himself as one of America's most distinguished authors and the most renowned farmer, people flocked to Malabar on the weekends to try and meet the man and his family behind the famous Malabar Farm in Pleasant Valley, Ohio. Bromfield often found himself speaking to crowds often approaching the number of 200, ranging from farmers and families to students wanting to learn Bromfield's method of farming. Bromfield would often spend all day with his guests and answer their questions about his farm. If a guest showed interest, Bromfield would invite them to stay and give them a room in the house. The room below, commonly referred to as 'The Red Room' is where he would gather with guests and friends staying at the house. During the evening, they would watch television here, and enjoy fine food and drinks until they retired to their quarters for the evening. The painting on the wall was done while they Bromfields lived in France. The Red Room was the original Parlor room.

"Clearly, it wasn't only a house; it was, despite its size, a home, what the French called a *foyer*. . ."
~Louis Bromfield.

Not only did Mary have her initials embroidered into her linen napkins, she also had them on her bed linens, as pictured below. This was the bedroom for Mrs. Bromfield. Mary and Louis slept separately and that can most likely be accredited to his erratic sleep schedule as he would sometimes stay up well into the night with guests or working on one of his several projects he seemed to always have. Bromfield also had letters coming in from around the world, so it is likely he would reply to those during the night. On September 14, 1952 Mary Appleton Wood Bromfield, 60, passed away in the Big House. She was in the bed below, which boasts ten of her husband's books on the headboard. Mary and Louis had been married for thirty one years. Her bedroom was the original living room to the house when the Herring family owned the land.

"I try to be conscientious about answering the letters of people who take the trouble to write, but it sometimes becomes physically impossible."
~Louis Bromfield.

Mr. Bromfield chose to have his room on the bottom floor of the Big House because he would often work late outside and then would come in to relax or read news papers or magazines. He also wanted easy access to his wife's room and to his best friend, editor, and manager's room, George Hawkins. Mary's bedroom was next door, and George's was just up the stairs. Mr. Bromfield's bed was right across the room from his oval desk, which was built by a local carpenter, Dwight Schumacher. If you pay close attention to the box at the end of his bed, you will see where his Boxer dogs once slept. This is where the nation's most beloved author, farmer, and politician would conduct his business and write his books, and most importantly reply to letters that people had written to him. Bromfield also had his class picture, and Pulitzer Prize hanging up in his bedroom as well.

"Afterward when it grew dark we all came to the Big House- men, women and children- where we sat very late gossiping and talking about farming at Malabar..."
~Louis Bromfield.

The Pugh Family.

On November 1, 1919 Georgia Mowery and Jim Pugh tied the knot. Georgia was born in Newville, Ohio on February 22, 1900. Newville is located within 15 miles of Malabar Farm. Due to the U.S. Army Corps of Engineers building a dam on the nearby Mohican River, the town was prone to flooding and was ordered to be evacuated, therefore, Newville no longer exists as a town, but only as a historical point in Richland County. Jim Pugh was born on June 27, 1892. The couple had their first born child, Robert Pugh, on February 5, 1922. Merely five years later their second child, Betty Pugh was born on February 15, 1926. Ten years after the family was together, Jim and Georgia Pugh bought land from a gentleman by the name of Mr. Beck in 1936. In 1938 Jim Pugh and his family built what is now known as Pugh Cabin. Throughout the summers of 1938 to 1947 the family lived in Mansfield and went to the cabin in the summers. However in 1947, the family put an addition on the cabin and moved into it. Mr. Pugh got hired in 1921 to work for the Ohio Edison electric company. Like most women who were wives and mothers at the time, Georgia stayed at home and took care of the home and children while the father and husband of the family went to work. By the time he retired, at age 67, he was the head of the line department for the Ohio Public Service. Jim dropped out of school in the eighth grade and read the entire encyclopedia of electricity. Jim was so fluent in electricity and the workings of it that he did not need electricity run to his home at Malabar farm; he managed to get power to his family's cabin from a water wheel that he had built at a nearby pond. The water wheel no longer exists, as modern electric methods have been implemented at the cabin. Since Jim Pugh was head of the line department for the Ohio Public Service, he had part of the decision of what happened when telephone line poles needed to be replaced. Jim thought he would take them and build a home. After years of stock piling, treating, and manufacturing every individual pole, that is exactly what he did, and that is how the famous Pugh Cabin came to be constructed, from de-commissioned telephone poles around the state of Ohio.

"Sometimes I should like to take to the woods and live the rest of my life in a cabin."
~Louis Bromfield.

Anne Chalmers Bromfield

Anne Bromfield was the first daughter to Louis and Mary Bromfield. She was also the only daughter to be born in the United States, as Hope and Ellen were born in France. The Bromfield daughters took very well after their parents enjoyment of entertaining, and doing it well, except for Anne. Anne was thought to have Autism as a child, and was anti-social and would have Schizophrenia set in as an adult. Anne would have to bear the unfortunate event of finding her mother, passed away in her room on that September day. Anne would also be the first daughter to pass away. The room below was used as a foyer area upstairs for the girls to socialize with their friends. The luxury of this room was that it was upstairs, separate from the adults and the girls could socialize together, with friends, without having to be around their parents.

"The usual busy weekend. Herbie Spencer and Dal, the two ensign friends of Hope, Came up as usual..."
~Louis Bromfield.

Mary Hope Bromfield

Mary Bromfield is the middle child of Mary and Louis. She was the first daughter born in France. She was born on June 27, 1929. In Bromfield's book, *Malabar Farm* Louis explains that Hope had friends from Columbus who came to stay the weekend before each left to go to the Atlantic and Pacific oceans to command destroyer escorts. Anne is the only daughter that went by her first name. Mary and Margaret went commonly by their middle names of Hope and Ellen. Below is Hope's bedroom. All the daughters had their own bedrooms with two beds; one for them and one for their guest. The room below is Hope's bedroom; however, Ellen and Anne had the same type of set up for theirs.

"It was good to be home again. I think sometimes that the farm is becoming an obsession to the exclusion of all else; which is bad, but there is in it so deep and so fundamental a satisfaction which is difficult to control."
~Louis Bromfield.

Margaret Ellen Bromfield

Margaret Ellen Bromfield was the last daughter that Louis and Mary had. She was born on April 25, 1932. Margaret would commonly be addressed by her middle name rather than her first name. She married Carson Geld, and the two moved to the Ceely Rose home on the Malabar property. She would live there while her husband, Carson, would serve in the United States Army. After Bromfield became friends with a businessman in Brazil, the couple moved to Brazil in hopes they would manage a farm much like Malabar. Carson and Ellen applied for the job and got hired. Louis told his daughter that he was "appalled" that she and Carson got the job. The farming operation in Brazil would be called *Fazenda Malabar-do-Brasil*. The farm would work closely with Louis to try and adopt the farming principals and practices. Carson and Ellen moved to Brazil to handle the farming operation in 1953. During their time there, they had a one year old son named, Steven, who was fluent in three different languages which included English, Italian, and Portuguese. Ellen was just twenty years old when she and Carson moved into Malabar-do-Brasil. Before long, Ellen was writing a weekly column for the local newspaper, while writing for one in the United States as well. Ellen also wrote for Brazilian women and agriculture publications. Bromfield described his grand son as "what his grandfather would like him to be- citizen not of one country but of the world." Bromfield was proud of Stevie because of his friends, who come from half a dozen of different nationalities. Ellen followed in her father's footsteps in two different aspects: writing and agriculture. At the age of twenty she was living in a foreign country, managing a farm that was modeled off her fathers, and she also wrote. Ellen authored books entitled, *Strangers In The Valley*, *The Jungley One*, *Brazil: Portrait of a Great Country*, *The Garlic Tree*, *A Timeless Place*, *The Dreamers*, and *A Winter's Reckoning*. *The Heritage* is about her memories of growing up on Malabar Farm in Ohio with her father, Louis Bromfield who was often referred to as 'The Boss'. Ellen and Carson still reside in Sao Paolo, Brazil.

"I see Malabar-do-Brasil as a project with possibilities of good and even high profits, having at the same time an influence for good upon the agricultural of Brazil..."
~Louis Bromfield.

Malabar-do-Brasil

The beginning of Malabar-do-Brasil traces back to the summer of 1941 when a pair of couples came to the Walnut tree in front of the big house and introduced themselves to Mr. Bromfield and wanted a tour of Bromfield's farm. Bromfield recalls that "they were intelligent" and that "they were interested." The couples were passing through from Chicago to New York and said that they had heard of Malabar and they wanted to stop by. There were several meetings between Bromfield and the owners of the land in Brazil before Bromfield and thirty five other Americans took two flights to Brazil via Braniff Airlines to visit the farm. Bromfield's company consisted of bankers, farmers, and livestock men. After those two significant trips, Bromfield took many more trips to Brazil to visit the friends he made there. In the years and trips to come, the farm in Brazil was started by a group of stockholders who included a gentleman named Carlito, who approached Louis in Ohio, and often was a liaison for his travels to Brazil. He also owned his own farm just forty-five minutes south of Malabar-do-Brasil. Another gentleman was a doctor whose formal name was Dr. Santos and a few other gentlemen, including Louis were stockholders, too. Louis also agreed to come to the farm in Brazil once a year, in the winter. The directors of the farming operation needed someone to assume the responsibilities of management on the premises. Bromfield plainly states his stance on the position by writing "virtually against my wishes, the directors moved in my daughter and son-in-law to undertake the management of the operation." During the first year of operation at Malabar-do-Brasil they focused on clearing dead trees and plants as well as trying to control erosion and soil depletion. However, the management and stockholders had an advantage compared to Bromfield when he started Malabar Farm. The farm in Brazil had some nice new barns and other buildings on the property as well as heavy duty equipment such as Caterpillar bulldozers. Within one year the soil was much richer and more fertile than that of Malabar Farm in one year's time. Within one year Louis was happy for his daughter and her family, as well as the operation in Brazil.

"I am very grateful to the Good Lord and to the Brazilian friends who made possible Malabar-do-Brasil where there is never a dull moment..."
~Louis Bromfield.

The Malabar Inn/Restaurant

David Schrack was born in Center County, Pennsylvania and moved to Ohio in 1819. He married Elizabeth Mogle and they had a family that consisted of twelve kids, three of which were boys: Charles, John, and David. The other nine were girls, Sarah, Catharine, Mary, Margaret, Elizabeth, Rachel, Sophia, Susan, and Ann. The family bought a section of land in Monroe Township from Mr. Thomas Pope where the family built a cabin until they could build what would be known today as the Malabar Inn, which currently houses the Malabar Farm Restaurant. The family lived here for about a year before building their large and comfortably accommodating home in 1820. The home stands along a now expired stage coach route between Sandusky and Marietta. The produce stand that sits east of the home has served as a hearty produce stand since the early 1950's. The stand was one of the most profitable (per acre) undertakings at Malabar, Bromfield explains in his book, *From My Experience*, published in 1955. The current roadside market was built a year after the original one. Once established, the idea was a wonderful hit with most local families making it a nice evening drive out to get their produce. By the next year contractors Ivan Bauer and Dwight Schumacher had plans for a "beautiful and airy pavilion with a whole brook of fresh spring water flowing through it." The contractors got the new stand done by June the next year. The roadside market also experienced shortages throughout the day. So, Bromfield had Mr. Schumacher design a storage shed that would be under ground so they would not have to put in a refrigeration unit, and later one was built so that all the workers of Malabar would have to do was walk across the road to the shed to restock produce versus keeping it in the field until they needed more. The storage shed also boasted a trough with running water so workers could store produce like crisp greens without any concern of them losing their color or crispiness. Workers could also bring an abundance of produce to the storage shed and wash it due to the troughs of cool fresh spring water flowing through all times of the year. To this day you can still buy fresh produce from the grounds of Malabar Farm.

"From the very beginning the business far exceeded all expectations. Despite the fact that the market stand was not located on a main highway..."
~Louis Bromfield.

What is known today as Mt. Jeez was known generations before Louis Bromfield's era as Poverty Knob. When Bromfield started farming this piece of land it was particularly rough. The hill contained plants such as poverty grass, broom sedge, sumac, blackberry bushes and goldenrod. When Bromfield started farming he decided the hill, over a mile away from his home, would be a great place to try and add inches of top soil. By the time Bromfield found the land it had been eroded and heavily farmed. That is when Bromfield and farmhands and managers assumed the task of re-vamping the land under the conditions that any regular farmer on a low budget could do. By the end of the year the hill contained plentiful, lush greens that could feed half a dozen cattle for a week. There is rumor that says the hill got renamed to Mt. Jeez after Bromfield took George Hawkins up the hill in one of his Jeeps and by the time they got to the top Hawkins was white knuckled and said "Jeez Louie!"

"Economically and philosophically I believe that good and productive soil is the very basis of man's existence, well-being and prosperity."
~Louis Bromfield.

The Main Barn at Malabar was the closest one to the Big House and housed the most important pieces of the ever evolving operation. The upper floor of the barn was used to store hay, straw, and farm equipment. The ground floor was where the livestock was kept. One of the first things Bromfield wanted to do was renovate the barns on the property to be able to accommodate modern machinery and to be able to correctly store hay and straw. Bromfield also had a greenhouse that he used to grow fresh herbs. The Main Barn is a timber frame barn, and was a common type of barn to use in hilly regions. This barn is called a "Bank Barn" and the reason is because this barn was built into the banks of hills, giving farmers the amenity of having what seemed to be two first floors. One floor was accessible from the front and the other floor was accessible from the back.

"Charley, like myself, is interested in the new dam proposed at Lexington. It will help the industrial water supply of Mansfield and create a beautiful new lake four miles long on the upper Clear Fork."
~Louis Bromfield.

Louis Bromfield initially was going to make Malabar a self-sufficient farm that would only support him and his family through WWII and beyond. In the spring that following year, 1939, Bromfield would realize that the land he had purchased was worse than he had initially realized. It was then that he would utilize his first farm manager, Max Drake, and his knowledge of agriculture to turn Malabar into a model farm for all. The plan for the farm was based off of two important, yet simple ideas; number one being that they would not do anything the average farmer could not do due to his lack of income or knowledge. The only raw materials that the farm would operate on would be grasses and grains. They would also utilize livestock and poultry and would market/sell beef, dairy products, pork, poultry products and all would be sold for a profit. Bromfield and Drake also agreed that the farm should not only be self sufficient but also diversified and that experiments with new methods of soil conservation be researched and implemented if they were feasible. The farm would also use and develop new methods of plowing using such equipment as the Chisel Plow, Graham Plow, Seaman Tiller, Ferguson Tiller, and Ferguson Offset Disk. Bromfield was passionate about restoring "Green Manures" which meant to restore nitrogen, lime, phosphorus, and potassium in the ground. The farm utilized several practices such as contour plowing, contour strips, crop rotation, grass waterways, French drains, farm ponds and woodlot management. Malabar would implement new innovations in the agriculture field such as trash mulching and horizontal silos. Two of the most notable practices at Malabar were the Reynolds Hay Barn and the multiflora rose bush. The hay barn was an all aluminum barn that was specially constructed off of the ground and had a unique design that allowed hay and other goods to stay dry through the damp Ohio season. The mulitflora rose bush was brought to the United States by Bromfield to eliminate the use of wooden fencing on farms. The rose bushes provided cover for animals; livestock could not pass through them and Bromfield saw it as a way to dress up the land while providing the luxuries of a wooden or steel fence. These bushes are known for spreading all over the country very quickly. Bromfield's top goal was to stop the destruction of soil by erosion and heal the gullies that almost every hill had on Malabar.

"The Clear Fork Valley is unbelievably beautiful with the steep wooded hills all about it, the lake mirroring the blue sky and the trees ranging in…"
~Louis Bromfield.

In the summer of 1896, Celia 'Ceely' Rose thought she found the love of her life. After being dubbed 'Silly' Rose, the locals knew there was something wrong with the girl, and she would justify their thoughts by the acts she would commit in the summer of 1896. Guy Berry, the neighbor boy, possessed a charming personality and was generous enough to stop and have a short conversation with Celia when he would see her. However, Guy was not as intimately interested in Celia, as she was in him. She became so fond of Guy that Guy's father had to confront David Rose and ask him to tell his daughter, Celia, to stay away from Guy. Celia was soon convinced that her family did not want her to see Guy. In Celia's eyes, if her family was gone she could continue living her life the way she wanted to. Little did she know, it was Guy's family who did not want them together.

Celia was born on March 13, 1873, in Pike County. Her family moved to the Pleasant Valley area in circa 1880. Celia's father, David, was born in 1829 in Highland County, Ohio to Lawrence and Thankful Reynolds Rose. Her mother, Rebecca Easter Rose was also born in 1834 in Highland County, Ohio to Jacob and Margaret Easter. Her brother, Walter Rose was born in 1856 in Highland County as well. Celia's love interest, Guy, was born to George and Angeline Berry in 1878 on September 12.

Celia and Guy went to school together as kids. In years to come, Celia would prove to be a constant interruption in Guy's work on the farm which is why David had to tell Celia to stay away from him. She became upset and decided to poison her father, mother, and brother. She would do so in the month of June 1896 on the twenty-fourth day in the morning. The poison that Celia used was called *Rough On Rats* which was an arsenic based product used to deter rats, mice, bed bugs, flies and cockroaches. She gave it to the family for breakfast with their cottage cheese (smear case). After breakfast, David and Walter went out to do their daily chores in the pastures and mills, while Rebecca and Celia stayed in and cleaned up after breakfast. Rebecca was the first to fall ill to the poison. When she did not feel well, she sent Celia to get her father. He rushed to the office of Dr.McCombs in Newville. Before the doctor and David could make it back to the Rose home, David felt too ill to continue the journey and had to be taken back

"I set off down the winding road past the cottage where Ceely Rose had poisoned her parents..."
~Louis Bromfield.

home via wagon. While the chaos was unfolding with the doctor, David, Rebecca, and Celia were in the home, while her brother, Walter, was yet to be found. He was thought to be okay until they found him, too ill to move, lying along the side of the road. While the doctor was helping escort Walter back home, Celia disposed of the smear case she used that morning at breakfast. Days later the neighbor, George Berry, found several of the Rose's chickens dead near the family's home. They most likely ate what Celia threw out just days earlier. David, Celia's father, would die six days later on June 30, 1896. Their son, Walter, succumbed to the poison on the Fourth of July. After losing her son and husband, Rebecca would actually start to show signs of improvement. When arsenic was found in David's stomach, and they confirmed it, Dr. Budd told Rebecca. Celia was in the other room and heard the conversation between the two. Later that day Rebecca told Celia to go get food for brunch and she returned promptly with what her mother asked. After enjoying her brunch, Rebecca took a nap and woke up with a mighty appetite. To help curb it, she told Celia to bring her leftovers from brunch. Celia was excited to give the leftovers to her mother, because before putting it away she put more of the poisoning, *Rough On Rats,* to help finish her mother off. Just hours later, her mother was on the floor, vomiting in every direction. It is quoted that her mother yelled at Celia, "Celia, if you have done this God help you!" She died later that day, July 19, 1896. Within the next month, Celia would admit to all the crimes. She made a confession on August 11, 1896 in a barn on the Ohler Farm, on Pleasant Valley Road. Celia was arrested the next day. She would then spend her days in a jail cell being questioned by lawyers and doctors. The lawyers worked closely with the doctors examining Celia to try and get proof that she was mentally unstable so they could use insanity as a defense. Celia drew quite the crowd to her jail cell and was often overwhelmed by the swarms of people. She got so overwhelmed that she would cover her head with an apron to avoid being seen. Trials began in October of that year. Celia was found not guilty and was acquitted (clear of charge) on the grounds of insanity. However, she was admitted to an insane asylum in Toledo. Celia was then transferred to Lima State Hospital. Celia would die years later in Athens on March 14, 1934.

"It was a *blue* winter night with that peculiar quality of blue in the sky and in the air itself."
~Louis Bromfield.

The Hostel on the grounds of Malabar Farm dates back to 1919, when it was built. The Hostel was an original Sears and Roebuck Co. Catalogue Order Home. Louis changed names for privacy. The house is now known as Hostelling International-Malabar Farm. It is on record that Mr. Bromfield did not like living in the house, however, during construction of the Big House, Mr. Bromfield was away in California writing screen plays. These kinds of homes were simply ordered from a Sears & Roebuck Co. catalogue and all the pre-cut pieces arrived by railroad and were delivered to the building site. Something so simple did not suit the lavish taste that Mr. Bromfield desired for his own home. Bromfield thought that the house looked like a home that belonged in the city, not in the country. When Louis would come home from Hollywood, walls in the big house were torn down and parts of the house were reconstructed to suite his needs and tastes. The house currently serves as a 21 bed hostel accommodating guests from all over the world.

"Each small experience is always new and exciting and filled with inner meaning."
~Louis Bromfield.

Not only did Louis Bromfield teach farmers down the road how to operate their farms, he also worked with notable people from all over the nation. Bromfield has been known to work with famous names affiliated with Hollywood and politics such as Tyrone Power, Lucille Ball, Humphrey Bogart, Lauren Bacall, Twentieth Century-Fox studios vice president, Darryl F. Zanuck, Republican Senator Robert A. Taft, Republican Congressman J. Harry McGregor, Mansfield mayor, Thomas B. Wright, scientist Albert Einstein and many more including Walt Disney and Shirley Temple, Ina Claire, the wife of James A. Farley, and actress Colleen Moore, who played in the 1934 film, *The Scarlet Letter*. The room below was designed by an employee of Walt Disney.

"A growing urban proletariat without economic security can wreck everything that America has been in the past and darken her whole future."
~Louis Bromfield.

Doris Duke was born on November 22, 1912 to James Buchanan Duke and Nanaline Holt Inman. She spent time at The Duke Family Farm in Somerville, New Jersey. Her father died in 1925 and left Doris and Nanaline millions of dollars as well as his estate. Her mother died in 1962. Doris' interest in horticulture inspired her to start Duke Gardens, which was an exotic public display of plants to honor her father. After Doris noticed that hundreds of Dutch Elm trees were dying along her estate's roads, she began to buy and read Bromfield's books. This led her to pursue a friendship with Louis Bromfield. Like many readers, reading the books were not enough so she decided to contact Bromfield, however, she was going to go about getting Bromfield's attention a little differently than most. She had her personal secretary send a letter letting Louis know that a plane was going to be sent for him to take him to the Duke Estate so he might tell Doris what she could do to save the trees. Upon receiving the letter, Louis simply ignored it. Astonished, she wrote a hand-written letter to Bromfield. In his frustration he replied and sent her a letter letting her know that they should be destroyed to prevent further loss of trees that might survive. Doris did not like the letter from Louis. Hearing about visitors from all over the world, Doris decided it was time to invite herself to Malabar to pay a visit to 'The Boss' about her trees. When she arrived at Malabar the rolling hills, green lavish fields, and hearty cattle took Doris by surprise. Her travel itinerary included a flight into Cleveland, Ohio then from there a private limousine would take her to Malabar Farm. Doris felt quite disconcerted about her vaunt arrival. After several visits she and Louis became quite close and is it documented that Doris wanted to become the next "Mrs. Bromfield." In Bromfield's later years his Scotch consumption increased immensely and Bromfield knew with each bottle of alcohol consumed, it would make it harder for his already swollen liver to handle. Louis did not know it, but Doris invested millions of dollars in research of medical treatments and even invested in the concept of a liver transplant. She worked with doctors and research teams at Duke Medical Center as well. Even if they would have found a cure or way to transplant a liver in time, Bromfield would have been anything but an easy-going patient.

"The conservatism of the farmer is sometimes his worst handicap."
~Louis Bromfield.

Louis had mentioned to friends that he had intentions on marrying Doris, but Malabar Farm had a $600,000 mortgage on it and Bromfield did not want others to think he was marrying Doris for her money. In order to help pay for medical treatment, Bromfield sold timber rights to trees on a certain portion of the farm but did not pay them off before he died in 1956 due to bone marrow cancer. Doris paid $11,500 to the A.W. Hinchcliff Company to buy back the rights, preventing the destruction of thousands of trees on the property. In recognition of her acts, the Doris Duke Trail now resides at Malabar Farm. The cave pictured below is behind the Pugh Cabin and can be found along the Butternut Trail.

"George, Mayo Bogart, Hope and Mac all left yesterday for the East for a couple days. The house gets to be more and more of a hotel with people going and coming."
~Louis Bromfield.

Not only did the Pugh Cabin give a home to the Pugh family, it also served as the home to banker Andy Dufrense from the ultra popular movie, *The Shawshank Redemption*. The cabin served as the opening scene for the movie. The Pugh cabin is located in the woods of the Malabar Farm State Park. Behind the cabin on the Butternut trail is what visitors refer to as 'The Cave at Malabar.' This cave was formed when the glaciers came into the Northern Ohio region during the last ice age. Residents of the cabin remember taking board games and playing them in the cave because it was significantly cooler than inside the cabin, which did not possess air conditioning. Caddy corner from the Pugh Cabin is the Sugar Shack. The Sugar Shack was built by the state of Ohio and is used to make maple Syrup from the many maple trees that are located on the farm. Bromfield often made maple syrup from the trees on his farm; however, Bromfield had a different place to make his maple syrup. The famous Pugh Cabin is available for rent for weddings, meetings, or a unique place to have your next family reunion.

"Tonight after the big rain the earth is steaming and a white cottony mist lay over the valley."
~Louis Bromfield.

The Schrack cemetery, which is also called Mount Olivet Cemetery or Bromfield Cemetery sits a top a grassy knoll on Bromfield's Malabar Farm. The cemetery is only 1/4 of an acre in size, but holds a lot of history dating back to pre Civil War. Civil War solider, George Franklin Baughman, died in St. Louis Missouri on March 24, 1863 and is buried here. Buried at The Schrack Cemetery are the Bromfield, Furguson, Fergueson, Tucker, Rider, Herring, Schrack, and Baughman families. On August 1, 1859 Charles and Susan Schrack sold the piece of land to Jacob Schrack for one dollar, which would be worth $27.78 according an inflation calculator in 2013. The grounds were to be used only "for the use of the citizens of this vicinity for common burial grounds." Louis Bromfield's mother, father, sister, and wife are all buried at the cemetery, as well as Bromfield himself, who was cremated. Bromfield's type of grave is referred to as a cenotaph, which is simply an empty grave. Jacob Schrack, who died on November 4, 1899 is also buried there.

"I built fences between the lower bluegrass pasture and the cemetery field. It was a brilliant day and that corner of the farm is one of the loveliest spots."
~Louis Bromfield.

As with my last book, *The Oho State Reformatory: An Overview* the last page was the page about the cemetery, so I planned this book to be the same. From this page and beyond you will see photos that I have taken and they did not make a spot in the previous sections in the book, or I was just exploring Malabar one day with a friend and decided to take photos. So, this next section has photos of Malabar that I have taken personally. They may be "raw" photos or they may be heavily photo-shopped. Please enjoy looking at the photos I have taken during the production of this book! Some photos do not have captions with them, so do. Some pictures do have text in them to describe what you are looking at.

Please ENJOY!

~Joe J.

Below is an original supper invitation sent to the Schumacher family from Malabar Farm.

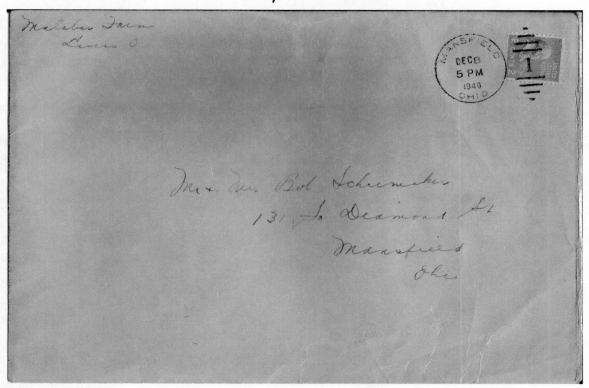

Supper Invitations to Malabar were common around the holidays, and to families that Bromfield had worked closely with.

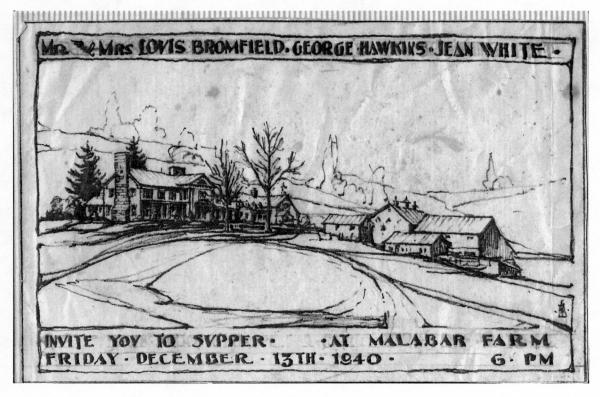

It is rumored that Bromfield was worried
about Doris Duke building an Olympic size pool
pictured in the hillside behind the Big House.

Back of Bromfield's Mansion.

Top: View pulling into Big House from driveway.

Louis Bromfield's Big House.

Bacall & Bogey's Honeymoon Suite.

Featured in " *Louis Bromfield and his Malabar Farm*" by Joe James
(C) 2013 Joe James

BIBLIOGRAPHY

"#78, 2 October 2006." *Louis Bromfield*. N.p., n.d. Web. 14 Mar. 2013.
<http://www.bookthink.com/0078/78lb1.htm>.

"AGAIN CALLS GIRL TO COURT.; Magistrate Resents the Failure of Woods's Cousin
to Appear." *AGAIN CALLS GIRL TO COURT*. New York TImes, 01 Nov. 1916. Web. 14
Mar. 2013.
<http://query.nytimes.com/gst/abstract.html?res=F10915FC3F5412738FDDA80894D941
5B868DF1D3>.

"Author Louis Bromfield, 59, Pulitzer Prize- Winner, Dies."
Http://news.google.com/newspapers. N.p., n.d. Web.
<http://news.google.com/newspapers?id=VLcxAAAAIBAJ&sjid=R-
QFAAAAIBAJ&pg=2203,523663&dq=louis+bromfield&hl=en>.

"Author Takes Acting Fling In Own Drama." *Http://news.google.com/newspapers*. N.p.,
n.d. Web.
<http://news.google.com/newspapers?id=g3wfAAAAIBAJ&sjid=MFcEAAAAIBAJ&pg
=6875,4163144&dq=louis+bromfield&hl=en>.

"Bradford Wins O. Henry Award." *Http://news.google.com/newspapers*. The Miami
News, n.d. Web.
<http://news.google.com/newspapers?id=vQcuAAAAIBAJ&sjid=MtgFAAAAIBAJ&pg
=6450,5590794&dq=louis+bromfield&hl=en>.

"Bromfield And Texas Chamber Feud Over Farm." *Http://news.google.com/newspapers*.
Ellensburg Daily Record, n.d. Web.
<http://news.google.com/newspapers?id=qoEKAAAAIBAJ&sjid=7ksDAAAAIBAJ&pg
=5199,2065483&dq=louis+bromfield&hl=en>.

"Bromfield Literary Career Reached Its Height In 1926."
Http://news.google.com/newspapers. N.p., n.d. Web.
<http://news.google.com/newspapers?id=p_tOAAAAIBAJ&sjid=tAAEAAAAIBAJ&pg
=7342,5454742&dq=louis+bromfield&hl=en>.

Bromfield, Louis. "Inflation Is Here Because President Chose Wrong Course."
Http://news.google.com/newspapers. Pittsburgh Post-Gazette, n.d. Web.
<http://news.google.com/newspapers?id=fQcwAAAAIBAJ&sjid=1GkDAAAAIBAJ&pg
=6387,2911970&dq=louis+bromfield&hl=en>.

Bromfield, Louis. "Some Rules for a Happy Marriage."
Http://news.google.com/newspapers. The Milwaukee Journal, n.d. Web.

<http://news.google.com/newspapers?id=07NQAAAAIBAJ&sjid=PyIEAAAAIBAJ&pg
=7012,2530454&dq=louis+bromfield&hl=en>.

Bromfield, Louis. "Voice From The Country." *Http://news.google.com/newspapers*.
Berkeley Daily Gazette, n.d. Web.
<http://news.google.com/newspapers?id=x0gyAAAAIBAJ&sjid=cOMFAAAAIBAJ&pg
=5918,3607955&dq=louis+bromfield&hl=en>.

"Erosion Peril to U.S. Cited." *Http://news.google.com/newspapers*. The Milwaukee
Sentinel, n.d. Web.
<http://news.google.com/newspapers?id=DFtQAAAAIBAJ&sjid=Ng4EAAAAIBAJ&pg
=6920,4768184&dq=louis+bromfield&hl=en>.

"Famed Novelist Louis Bromfield Succumbs At 59."
Http://news.google.com/newspapers. N.p., n.d. Web.
<http://news.google.com/newspapers?id=LotIAAAAIBAJ&sjid=_nUDAAAAIBAJ&pg=
3493,2205726&dq=louis+bromfield&hl=en>.

"Final Arguments Slated In Bromfield Farm Suit." *Http://news.google.com/newspapers*.
The Victoria Advocate, n.d. Web.
<http://news.google.com/newspapers?id=JcgcAAAAIBAJ&sjid=eFoEAAAAIBAJ&pg=
1715,3250370&dq=louis+bromfield&hl=en>.

"For Farm Strike." *Http://news.google.com/newspapers*. Lawrence Journal-World, n.d.
Web.<http://news.google.com/newspapers?id=81leAAAAIBAJ&sjid=FmENAAAAIBAJ
&pg=1278,4735539&dq=louis+bromfield&hl=en>
.

"Highlights of a Life." *WOSU Presents Ohioana Authors*. N.p., n.d. Web. 14 Mar. 2013.
http://www.ohioana-authors.org/bromfield/highlights.php
.

"Jaundice Virus Kills Author." *Http://news.google.com/newspapers*. N.p., n.d. Web.
<http://news.google.com/newspapers?id=dpcpAAAAIBAJ&sjid=hckEAAAAIBAJ&pg=
4852,2839628&dq=louis+bromfield&hl=en>.

"Louis Bromfield, Author, Dies of Liver Ailment." *Http://news.google.com/newspapers*.
N.p., n.d. Web.
<http://news.google.com/newspapers?id=XlpHAAAAIBAJ&sjid=YP4MAAAAIBAJ&p
g=2213,1870137&dq=louis+bromfield&hl=en>.

"Louis Bromfield Dies; Famed Author, Farmer." *Http://news.google.com/newspapers*.
N.p., n.d. Web.
<http://news.google.com/newspapers?id=too_AAAAIBAJ&sjid=bFUMAAAAIBAJ&pg
=680,1546132&dq=louis+bromfield&hl=en>.

"Louis Bromfield Hits Chamber's 'Sniping'" *Http://news.google.com/newspapers*. The Modesto Bee, n.d. Web. <http://news.google.com/newspapers?id=eAsuAAAAIBAJ&sjid=FIAFAAAAIBAJ&pg=3218,2468553&dq=louis+bromfield&hl=en>.

"Louis Bromfield." *Http://news.google.com/newspapers*. N.p., n.d. Web. <news.google.com/newspapers?id=t4o_AAAAIBAJ&sjid=bFUMAAAAIBAJ&pg=6891,1727279&dq=louis+bromfield&hl=en>.

"Louis Bromfield The Farmer's Plight Is As Hard As Ever." *Http://news.google.com/newspapers*. The Miami News, n.d. Web. <http://news.google.com/newspapers?id=x0MyAAAAIBAJ&sjid=h-cFAAAAIBAJ&pg=3882,1743359&dq=louis+bromfield&hl=en>.

"Louis Bromfield's Father Is Dead." *Http://news.google.com/newspapers*. Pittsburgh Post-Gazette, n.d. Web. <http://news.google.com/newspapers?id=0aYkAAAAIBAJ&sjid=uGkDAAAAIBAJ&pg=1726,5461064&dq=charles+bromfield&hl=en>.

"Malabar Farm State Park: Ohio State Parks - Historical Timeline." *Malabar Farm State Park: Ohio State Parks*. N.p., n.d. Web. 14 Mar. 2013. <http://www.malabarfarm.org/index.php/top-attractions/historical-timeline>. McIntyre, O.O.

"New York Day By Day." *Http://news.google.com/newspapers*. The Miami News, n.d. Web. <http://news.google.com/newspapers?id=FS8uAAAAIBAJ&sjid=3NUFAAAAIBAJ&pg=3745,4577960&dq=louis+bromfield&hl=en>.

"Mother of Author Dies at His Home." *Http://news.google.com/newspapers*. Palm Beach Daily News, n.d. Web. <http://news.google.com/newspapers?id=RoIhAAAAIBAJ&sjid=eosFAAAAIBAJ&pg=6812,5491406&dq=annette+coulter+bromfield&hl=en>.

"New Peace Plan." *Http://news.google.com/newspapers*. St. Petersburg Times, n.d. Web. <http://news.google.com/newspapers?id=Y_lOAAAAIBAJ&sjid=Vk4DAAAAIBAJ&pg=2409,4747906&dq=louis+bromfield&hl=en>.

"New-York Tribune., October 13, 1921, Page 11, Image 11About New-York Tribune. (New York [N.Y.]) 1866-1924." *News about Chronicling America RSS*. N.p., n.d. Web. 14 Mar. 2013.

"No Short-Cuts to Peace." *Http://news.google.com/newspapers*. The Pittsburgh Press, n.d. Web.

<http://news.google.com/newspapers?id=QwAiAAAAIBAJ&sjid=G04EAAAAIBAJ&pg=1694,5677239&dq=louis+bromfield&hl=en>.

"Ohio Reading Road Trip | Louis Bromfield Biography." *Ohio Reading Road Trip | Louis Bromfield Biography*. N.p., n.d. Web. 14 Mar. 2013. <http://www.orrt.org/bromfield/>.

"Our Walker's DeLuxe Butler Turns a Phrase for Louis Bromfield." *Http://news.google.com/newspapers*. N.p., n.d. Web. <http://news.google.com/newspapers?id=n2QrAAAAIBAJ&sjid=uNkEAAAAIBAJ&pg=938,1694327&dq=louis+bromfield&hl=en>.

Richert, Earl. "Margarine Would Grase Skids, Bring Communism, Bromfield Says." *Http://news.google.com/newspapers*. The Pittsburgh Press, n.d. Web. <http://news.google.com/newspapers?id=dvYaAAAAIBAJ&sjid=O00EAAAAIBAJ&pg=2760,1433932&dq=louis+bromfield&hl=en>.

Robb, Inez. "3 Cars In Every Garage As Inez Robb Discovers America." The Miami News, n.d. Web. <http://news.google.com/newspapers?id=ZFszAAAAIBAJ&sjid=ougFAAAAIBAJ&pg=2536,2377142&dq=malabar+farm&hl=en>.

"Soil Conserving Voters to Pass Conference Set on School Levy." *Http://news.google.com/newspapers*. The Spokesman-Review, n.d. Web. http://news.google.com/newspapers?id=w3pWAAAAIBAJ&sjid=oeUDAAAAIBAJ&pg=6842,6083666&dq=louis+bromfield&hl=en
.

"Weather May Be Changed By New Lakes in Ohio." *Http://news.google.com/newspapers*. The Pittsburgh Press, n.d. Web. <http://news.google.com/newspapers?id=PRQhAAAAIBAJ&sjid=144EAAAAIBAJ&pg=2095,1976853&dq=louis+bromfield&hl=en>.

Welsh-Huggins, Andrew. "Farm Founded by Novelist Bromfield Celebrates 60 Years." *Http://news.google.com/newspapers*. Rome News-Tribune, n.d. Web. <http://news.google.com/newspapers?nid=348&dat=19991017&id=73AwAAAAIBAJ&sjid=PjUDAAAAIBAJ&pg=6722,5178410>.

"Wife Of Noted Author Dies." *Http://news.google.com/newspapers*. St. Petersburg Times, n.d. Web. <http://news.google.com/newspapers?id=iaBaAAAAIBAJ&sjid=HE8DAAAAIBAJ&pg=3512,154005&dq=mary+appleton+wood+bromfield+death&hl=en>.

"Writers United Against Authors' Authority." *Http://news.google.com/newspapers*. N.p., n.d. Web. <http://news.google.com/newspapers?id=fGRSAAAAIBAJ&sjid=vXwDAAAAIBAJ&pg=5479,955263&dq=louis+bromfield&hl=en>.

Bromfield, Louis, and Kate Lord. *Pleasant Valley*. New York: Harper & Brothers, 1945. Print.

Bromfield, Louis. *From My Experience: The Pleasures and Miseries of Life on a Farm*. New York, NY: Harper & Bros., 1955. Print.

Bromfield, Louis. *Malabar Farm;*. New York: Harper, 1948. Print.

Carter, John T. *Louis Bromfield and the Malabar Farm Experience*. Mattituck, NY: Amereon House, 1995. Print.

Duke, Pony, and Jason Thomas. *Too Rich: The Family Secrets of Doris Duke*. New York: HarperCollins, 1996. Print.

Geld, Ellen Bromfield. *The Heritage; a Daughter's Memories of Louis Bromfield*. New York: Harper, 1962. Print.

THANK YOU

The publication of this book would have never been possible if was not for the help of many people such as my parents as they have always supported me with everything I have done. My grandparents and step-grandparents have always been supportive and encouraging of all my decisions in the endeavors that I choose to do. I would like to thank Nick Gaumer's parents; Mike and Carrie, for letting me dedicate this book to their son. The wonderful picture of Nick in the front of the book was taken by Zan Holt, and it is greatly appreciated that she has allowed the photo to be used in this book. Author and Playwright, Mark Jordan, is the editor of the book and he has done a great job editing it. Donna Bence has also put in countless hours of proof-reading the entire manuscript and being an honest critic of this book before the official publication. Matthew Davies has done a wonderful job on the cover and it would not look as nice as it does with out his knowledge and patience. Greg Seiter was quick to write the sincere forward in the book and it is highly appreciated that he agreed to do so. My friends have given me an abundant amount of support and ambition through the publication process and continue to do so even after. A very special thanks goes to The staff at Malabar Farm, The Ohio Genealogical Society, and The John Sherman Room at the Mansfield/Richland County Public Library, who all have been instrumental in helping provide me with all of the information I needed to write this book.

Thank you for purchasing and reading my book. I hope you gathered many interesting facts and stories from this book. Please don't forget to check out my other book, *The Ohio State Reformatory: An Overview*, and to keep an eye out for the next!
-Joe James.